HITTING

THE
WINNING
EDGE

HITTING

By BOB CLUCK

Foreword by RYNE SANDBERG

CONTEMPORARY
BOOKS, INC.
CHICAGO • NEW YORK

Library of Congress Cataloging-in-Publication Data

Cluck, Bob.
  The winning edge : hitting.

  1. Batting (Baseball)—Juvenile literature.
I. Title.
GV869.C55   1987   796.357'26   86-32940
ISBN 0-8092-4786-0 (pbk.)

All photos courtesy Teri Cluck Photography
Equipment courtesy San Diego School of Baseball

Published by Contemporary Books, Inc.
180 North Michigan Avenue, Chicago, Illinois 60601
Manufactured in the United States of America
Library of Congress Catalog Card Number: 86-32940
International Standard Book Number: 0-8092-4786-0

Published simultaneously in Canada by Beaverbooks, Ltd.
195 Allstate Parkway, Valleywood Business Park
Markham, Ontario L3R 4T8 Canada

*To Teri, Jennifer, and Amber
for patience during the long road trips
and the film sessions at home
over 20 great years*

Contents

Foreword

What makes a good major league baseball hitter? Good bat speed, eye contact, or concentration? Many people have their favorite approaches to good hitting; however, my work as a good hitter began as a young boy.

As a young Little Leaguer, I concentrated on the fundamentals demonstrated by my coaches. They taught me everything from the proper hitting stance to eye-hand coordination. These teachings took a lot of practice and a great deal of time commitment. I realized that good hitters are not born every day; they must work long and hard to reach their goals. Good hitting is a combination of good coaching, practicing the fundamentals, and a strong desire to work toward a goal.

Don't ever be afraid to ask a coach or friend for help on hitting. This will help you reach your goal a lot quicker and strengthen your foundation of becoming a good hitter.

Good luck and keep practicing!

Ryne Sandberg
Chicago Cubs

1
What to Do Before You Hit

BAT SELECTION

Hitters of all ages, from Little Leaguers to Major
Leaguers have a tendency to use too big a bat.
Studies have shown that a hitter is more efficient
with a lighter bat. One of the most productive
hitters in recent years who uses a light bat is 1984
batting champion Tony Gwynn. Tony's bat is 32½
inches long and weighs 30 ounces, which makes it
one of the smallest in major league history. The
name of the game is bat control, and if you use a
bat that is too heavy, you're kidding yourself. It
begins when you emulate a major league star or
an older brother who is bigger and stronger. It
becomes a "macho" thing with some hitters who
feel they must use a big bat to be a "big" hitter.
Using a heavy bat can cause a variety of me-

chanical problems—among them poor vision, bad balance, slow bat speed, and a poor path of the bat head to the ball. Defects can develop that will permanently scar a young hitter, defects that can be difficult to correct.

REASONS YOU SHOULDN'T USE A HEAVY BAT

▶ A big bat is difficult to control and will cause you to strike out more.
▶ A big bat forces you to use more upper body to swing and makes your front side pull off the ball.
▶ If you are not strong enough for the bat you are using, you will have poor bat speed and will not be able to hit the ball hard.
▶ Mechanical chain reactions develop that can damage your swing and make it difficult to correct.

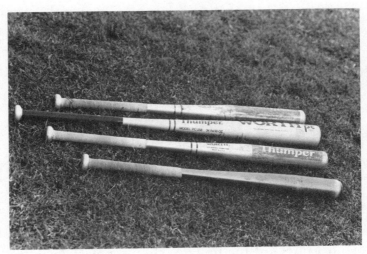

A variety of aluminum bats is available to hitters of all ages, pick one that feels "too light."

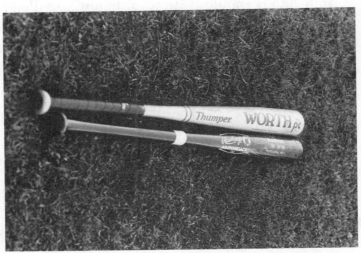

Batting champion Tony Gwynn's bat is one of the smallest in the major leagues.

THE PROPER GRIP

Many baseball players and coaches are confused about what is the correct grip on a baseball bat. Some will tell you to line up your knuckles one way or the other, and others will tell you it doesn't matter.

You must find your own grip by a simple process. Place the bat in front of you as if it were an ax. Lay the bat handle at the joint where the fingers meet the hands, and close your hands around the bat handle. Bring the bat up and you have the proper grip for you. It doesn't matter how your knuckles line up. You should never place the bat back in your palm. You will not be able to control the bat if it is in the fatty tissue of your hand.

Your hands should be in what might be called a "firm/relaxed" position while you wait for the pitch. By gripping the bat too tightly, you restrict the muscles of your hands, forearms, and arms. Restricted muscles cannot move quickly and effectively. Your hands will automatically firm up when the bat approaches contact with the ball.

What to Do Before You Hit

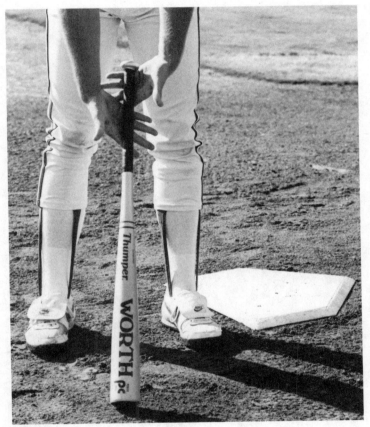

Place the bat on the ground in front of you and put the bat handle at the joint where your fingers meet your hand.

Close your hands around the bat handle, and when you bring the bat up you will have the proper grip for you.

It doesn't matter how your knuckles line up, as long as you are comfortable.

The bat shouldn't be back in your palm, because you will lose bat control.

A BALANCED, WORKABLE STANCE

When you assume a stance in the batter's box, you are establishing a position from which you will perform the world's most difficult skill. Some thought should be given to how you are going to stand, and there should be good reason for the position. It doesn't matter where you position your hands; great hitters have held their hands in a variety of positions. The bottom line is that it should be comfortable for you, with your feet about shoulder-width apart.

The initial position is simply the position from which you start all of your preliminary movements. It is a base to work from and should contain certain fundamentals. First, you should have "plate coverage." That simply means that you can hit the ball on the outside corner with a normal effort.

Your head position should be such that you can see the pitcher clearly with both eyes.

The third point (and maybe the most important) is that your stance should not be a copy of someone else's but yours and yours alone. A stance that is workable and comfortable for a major league star might not work or be comfortable for you.

Keep in mind that you don't swing the bat from the initial position. The stride and other events must take place before the swing begins. Your hands will move (trigger) the bat to the hitting position before the bat starts forward.

HITTING

There are four basic stances hitters use: the "closed" stance, the "straightaway" stance, the "open" stance, and the "slightly closed" stance. The most common of these and the one most recommended is the "slightly closed" stance.

The "closed" stance used by Garry Templeton and other major leaguers.

The "open" stance used by Brian Downing and others.

Many big league players, Gary Carter, for instance, use this "straightaway" stance.

The "slightly closed" stance used by hitting stars such as Steve Garvey, Tony Gwynn, and George Brett is the one most often recommended.

A simple check for plate coverage involves assuming the position after the stride (the hitting position), and reaching across home plate with a normal effort and touching the outside corner with the bat.

JUST BE COMFORTABLE

Every hitter has a stance that "feels right." There's no right or wrong way to hold your hands—some of the greatest hitters have had some of the most unusual stances.

Pete Rose's stance is unusual, but he's had more hits than any other player in the history of baseball.

Steve Garvey's famous stance has given him the reputation of consistency and reliability at the plate.

Carl Yastrzemski collected more than 3,400 hits (seventh on baseball's all-time list) for the Boston Red Sox with this stance.

Hall-of-Famer Stan Musial, third on the all-time hit list, had more than 3,600 hits from his unique stance.

2
Improving Your Swing and Hitting

SEEING THE BALL CLEARLY

Nothing is more important to a hitter than seeing the ball. Clear vision is the base from which you work. If anything in your swing hinders your seeing the ball, it must be eliminated.

The most common flaw among young hitters is trying to hit the ball too hard. This makes the front side rotate away from the ball, and the head follows. Once your head moves, your eyes cannot focus clearly on the ball. You must keep your head still to hit the ball with any consistency.

If you make an effort to keep your head down as you swing, chances are you will see the ball well. Keep in mind that this is a recurring problem that can only be controlled and never eliminated. Everyone swings too hard at times; it is human nature to try to do more than you are capable of doing. As you mature and develop, you should be able to take a full swing and keep overall balance and control. This is a learned and trainable skill. Young hitters can learn to control their swing and cut it down to a workable tempo.

When you swing too hard, it disrupts your overall balance, and prevents you from seeing the ball clearly.

Improving Your Swing and Hitting

Focus on the ball as soon as possible as you watch the pitcher. When the ball approaches the release point, focus on the point at which it will be released. Although most pitchers throw all of their pitches from the same arm position, some throw overhand, some three-quarter, and some sidearm.

Focus on the pitcher's release point. This pitcher is throwing overhand.

Most pitchers throw all their pitches (fastball, curveball, etc.) from the same arm position. This pitcher is pitching from the most common arm position, which is three-quarter.

This pitcher is throwing sidearm; it is usually easiest to see the ball from this arm position.

USING THE HANDS PROPERLY

A hitter uses his hands to get the bat to the baseball. During the initial stance, hold your hands in a comfortable position. When the stride begins, your hands start to "trigger." This means that the hands move from the comfortable starting position to the hitting position. Although the intitial position is an individual thing, *the hitting position is nearly the same for every hitter who has ever lived.*

The hitting position is about shoulder high and in the area of the armpit. This is the position from which you move the bat forward toward the ball. Your hands arrive at this position at the same time your stride foot is planted. The motion that the hands make from initial to hitting position is called the "trigger" or "cocking action."

Many hitters such as Hank Aaron, Dave Winfield, Keith Hernandez, and others drop their hands and bring them back up to trigger them. Some people call this a "hitch," but this is nothing more than a natural movement by the hitter to put the bat in motion. A dead weight is hard to move quickly, but that same weight (the bat) in motion is easy to move. Young hitters with a "trigger" that makes their hands go down first are doing a great job moving the bat and shouldn't be told to stop "hitching."

Your hands may drop first, but as long as they return to shoulder level (approximately), this movement is just an effective "trigger."

Your hands arrive at the hitting position at the same time you plant your stride foot.

Improving Your Swing and Hitting

The hands must get the head of the bat on the path of the ball and leave it there for as long as possible. As the hands begin to move to the ball, they pass close to the body. They will extend out from there and actually lead the bat head toward the ball at the beginning of the swing. This is what is commonly called an *inside out swing*. It is the most common and effective swing in baseball. The bottom arm (left hand for a right-handed hitter) must not take an upward path during the early stages of the swing. The bottom arm must be forced downward to insure a level swing. If the bottom arm flies upward, the bat head will begin (and finish) the swing below the hands. This inefficient movement is called a *chicken wing*. It is a common problem among hitters of all ages and can only be controlled with lots of work and patience.

The bat continues toward the ball and stays on the plane of the ball unless something happens to bring the bat off that plane.

Keep your hands close to your body during the early stages of the swing.

When the bottom elbow rides upward, the bat head will always be below the hands, resulting in an inefficient swing called a "chicken wing."

THE STRIDE, THE HIPS, WEIGHT TRANSFER, AND EXTENSION

THE STRIDE

As the hands "trigger" the bat, the stride puts the body in motion to do its job. The stride should be a soft step in the direction of the pitcher. If it becomes a jumping motion the stride foot lands on the heel and problems develop.

▶ When your stride foot lands too hard, it makes your eyes move and vision is disturbed.
▶ Your stride should be short enough so that you don't land on your heel.
▶ If your stride foot lands on the heel, then you will rotate or "spin off" the ball.
▶ Your stride foot should open about 45 degrees.
▶ It is important that the toe of your stride foot doesn't open too much, or your weight will be trapped on the back side.

Your stride should be a controlled, easy step toward the pitcher.

If your stride is too long, you will land on your heel and cause mechanical problems in your swing.

It is important that the toe of your stride foot not open too much.

The correct angle for your stride foot is about 45 degrees.

THE HIPS

The hips free the hands to get through the ball, and they help in the weight transfer. They do not play the important role many people believe they do. Find a hitter who "pops his hips open" and you'll have a hitter who comes "off" the ball, doesn't see the ball well, and has lots of slumps. There is no question that the hips need to open for a workable swing, but as part of the weight transfer, not as a violent movement.

WEIGHT TRANSFER

It is important that weight transfer be smooth and consistent. It begins with the stride, and as the back side (rear hip) comes through, the weight is transferred to the front side (the stride foot). Your body weight travels forward until it meets resistance against the front side. You then block against this firm front leg and create the necessary leverage. This leverage allows you to deliver a powerful blow to the ball. The front leg must remain firm (but not stiff) for maximum leverage.

EXTENSION

To achieve "extension," you must reach out and extend through the ball as you hit it. A great place to work on this is the tee. The more extension you have in your swing, the more efficiently you're going to hit the ball. Remember your wrists shouldn't roll over until after contact.

Your front leg should remain firm, but not stiff, so your body can block against it for leverage.

If your front leg collapses, you won't have leverage, and therefore you won't have power.

DRILLS FOR DEVELOPING AND MAINTAINING A GOOD SWING

Hitting is a difficult skill that requires lots of practice. In order to develop a good swing, you must dedicate yourself to this end. Swinging the bat as much as possible is a step in the right direction. Several drills will help to attain this goal.

HITTING OFF THE TEE

When using the batting tee, place it well out in front. Contact is made with the ball in front of the plate, and it's important that the tee be in the right place. The ball should be moved around to cover the inside corner, the outside corner, and the middle of the plate. High and low pitches should also be included in the workout.

One of the greatest things about a tee is that you don't need anyone else to practice. Tees are inexpensive and most people can even build one. By using whiffle balls you can get hundreds of quality swings a week in the backyard or garage in summer or winter.

Make an effort to keep the ball out of the air while hitting off the tee. Hard grounders and line drives should be the goal. The tee is the best place to develop a good swing and maintain one after you have developed one.

Place the ball well out in front to make the contact point realistic. Notice how far out in front this inside pitch is being hit.

When the ball is on the outside corner, it is hit farther back toward home plate.

THE "SOFT TOSS" OR "BALL TOSS" DRILL

This drill is done with the help of another person. The "feeder" throws balls underhanded to you in different areas. This drill allows you to follow the ball and time its flight. The feeder should move the ball to different areas without you knowing in advance. High and low pitches should be mixed in as the drill proceeds.

The "toss" drill can improve your coordination because it makes you time the flight of the ball.

When you're doing this drill, notice that the ball is thrown out in front of the plate to simulate actual contact.

HITTING THE BALL THE OTHER WAY

When you are serious about becoming the best hitter you can be, you need to develop good practice habits. One of the best ways to enhance hitting skills is by hitting the ball the other way. When a right-handed hitter hits the ball to right field, he is almost always using good mechanics.

When you hit the ball the other way, you naturally keep your head down, and watch the ball longer. You will seldom overswing, and you will have good balance on most swings when you're hitting to right field.

By keeping the hands in front of the bat head for a longer time, and by letting the ball get closer to him, the hitter can successfully hit the ball the other way. A good way to learn this skill is to hit balls off the tee on the outside corner.

HITTING GROUND BALLS TO THE INFIELDERS

By hitting grounders to the infielders in practice, you develop a downward stroke that will help you keep the bat level through the swing.

3
Solving Your Hitting Problems

PROBLEM 1
You step in the bucket, and pull away from the pitch with your front side.

SYMPTOMS OF THE PROBLEM

- You have poor balance.
- You're swinging at many bad pitches.
- You're having trouble seeing the ball clearly.
- Your stride foot lands on the heel.
- You rarely hit the ball on the outside half of the plate hard.

POSSIBLE SOLUTIONS

▶ Hit off the tee, with the ball placed on the extreme outside corner. Hit to the opposite field and don't pull the ball.

HITTING

- ▶ Hit everything up the middle on the ground when taking batting practice.
- ▶ Move away from the plate six to eight inches to force you to stride toward the ball.

Don't stride away from the pitch or many problems will develop.

Always stride toward the pitcher, with your weight on the ball of your stride foot.

PROBLEM 2
You're striking out too much.

SYMPTOMS OF THE PROBLEM

- You swing at everything.
- You miss balls "right down the middle."
- You lack confidence.
- You don't see the ball clearly out of the pitcher's hand, it is never in focus.

POSSIBLE SOLUTIONS

▶ Cut down on your swing and try to hit balls on the ground in practice.
▶ Use the batting tee or hit against a pitching machine at a slow speed to build confidence.
▶ Have your eyes checked.
▶ To fight a negative attitude, think about the good things you've done as a hitter in the past.
▶ Use a bat of lighter weight.

If you strike out too much, it usually means you're overswinging or using a bat that is too heavy for you.

PROBLEM 3
You have trouble with off-speed pitches.

SYMPTOMS OF THE PROBLEM

- You jump out onto your stride foot.
- You seem to "reach" for everything.
- You have poor balance on most swings.

POSSIBLE SOLUTIONS

▶ Hit everything to the opposite field during practice (this problem will not go away but can only be controlled with hard work).
▶ Hit off the tee and try to improve your weight transfer and timing.

If you're fooled by off-speed pitches consistently, that usually means you have an erratic weight transfer.

By working with the tee and hitting the ball to the opposite field, you can improve against off-speed pitches.

PROBLEM 4
You have a severe uppercut.

SYMPTOMS OF THE PROBLEM

- You never hit the ball above the waist hard.
- Your hips are not rotating fully.
- Your back leg collapses on every swing.
- No weight transfer is present.
- Your back shoulder is lower than the front.

POSSIBLE SOLUTIONS

▶ Hit off the tee with the ball placed letter high, and hit everything on the ground.

▶ Place the ball on the tee waist high and hit the ball by chopping down with just your top hand (only) on the bat (right hand for right-handed hitter).

▶ Work in the area of the hips and the weight transfer.

If you have a severe uppercut, your back leg will collapse on every swing.

By hitting off the tee with just the top hand, you can help eliminate an uppercut.

PROBLEM 5
You have insufficient rotation of hips.

SYMPTOMS OF THE PROBLEM

- You lose your balance after you swing.
- Your back foot slides forward instead of pivoting.
- You never seem to pull the ball.
- The toe of your stride foot is opening too far.

POSSIBLE SOLUTIONS

▶ Improve your weight transfer by hitting down on the ball off the tee and in practice.
▶ Stride with the toe closed and practice this with a hundred simulated swings a day.
▶ Lean forward (over the plate) slightly when practicing simulated swings, and finish your swing by having your weight finish over your front foot (you should look down after you swing, and your head should be over your front foot).

This hitter has a good pivot with the rear foot and a beautiful weight transfer.

PROBLEM 6
You're late on everything.

SYMPTOMS OF THE PROBLEM

- You never seem to pull the ball, even on off-speed pitches.
- You're constantly getting "jammed" (hit near the hands on the bat).
- You hit lots of pop-ups, mostly to the right side of the field (if you're right-handed).

POSSIBLE SOLUTIONS

▶ Try a bat two or three ounces lighter.
▶ Check your grip (an incorrect grip can make you late on everything).
▶ Hit off the tee with just the bottom arm (left hand for a right-handed hitter) and try to hit the ball on the ground to the third baseman.

Hitting off the tee with the bottom hand will improve the angle of your bat coming through the strike zone (you should be trying to hit the ball to an imaginary third baseman).

PROBLEM 7
You're having trouble with the outside pitch.

SYMPTOMS OF THE PROBLEM

- You're stepping into the bucket (away from the pitcher).
- You may be standing too far from the plate.
- You hit lots of weak grounders up the middle.
- You take a lot of strikes on the outside corner and claim they aren't strikes.

POSSIBLE SOLUTIONS

▶ Check your plate coverage and move closer if necessary.
▶ Place the ball on the tee and hit 50 balls a day to right field.
▶ Stop trying to pull the ball and don't swing too hard.

4
Executing in Game Situations

MAN ON SECOND, NO OUTS

In this situation, you need to hit the ball on the ground to the right side of the field. This will advance the runner to third base with just one out (assuming you're thrown out at first). The runner now has an excellent chance to score a run.

Be patient and wait for a good pitch to hit to the right side of the field. Although almost any pitch can be hit to right by an experienced hitter, it is easier with a ball out over the plate. If you're a left-handed hitter, you have an easier job. One of the easiest skills in hitting is pulling the ball on the ground.

Experienced pitchers in this situation will keep

the ball in on right-handed hitters and away from the left-handers.

This is not a sacrifice situation and you shouldn't just "punch" the ball to the second baseman. Coaches won't object if you hit the ball hard to the opposite field to drive in the run with no outs.

MAN ON THIRD, ONE OUT OR NO OUTS

Your job in this situation is simple: score the runner any way you can.

In a close game with the tying or winning run on third, the only thing a coach hates to see is a strikeout. You must battle the pitcher and put the ball in play. If you must choke up or cut down on your swing then that is your job.

In the major leagues, hitters will try to get the ball in the air to drive in the run with a sacrifice fly. For younger hitters this is not a good plan. The inexperienced hitter should simply try to hit the ball hard and let the results take care of themselves.

HIT-AND-RUN PLAY

In a hit-and-run situation, you must swing at anything. You can't take the pitch under any circumstances, because the runner is running with the pitch and must be protected. Too many hitters try to hit the ball the opposite way on a hit-and-run play. This isn't necessary, because a grounder anywhere will do the job. Major leaguers will even switch off the coverage from time to time just to disrupt the good hit-and-run men in the league

You should practice the hit-and-run play both as a hitter and as a runner. You may possibly be called on to hit a ball way out of the strike zone to protect the runner. Because hitting this kind of pitch is unnatural, it must be practiced. The runner also needs to practice the timing of the play.

5
Practice, Practice, Practice

So now you've learned the fundamentals, but what are you going to do with your new knowledge? If you really do want to be the best on the field, you've got to practice—it isn't going to be automatic. There are hundreds of big leaguers who got to where they are today because they made a commitment to being the best, and being the best means putting your heart into it.

Here are some ways you can make practice easier.

▶ Set aside a certain time every day to just practice hitting.
▶ Get a friend or parent or coach to help you and tell you if you're doing it right.
▶ Don't give up! Stick with it and the time you spend practicing will pay off.

HITTING

The most important thing is that you never give up. Everyone who has ever played the game of baseball has had slumps and problems, and you might, too. But hard work and discipline will help you overcome those rough times, and send you on your way to being the best ballplayer you can be!

Index

HITTING

Index